EMPOWERED:
A CANCER GUIDE TO HEALING, SURVIVING, AND FEELING BETTER

ADELAIDE C. LENOX

Illustrations by Kinley Donaldson   Photographs by Adelaide Lenox

Balboa Press books may be ordered through booksellers or by contacting:

Balboa Press
A Division of Hay House
1663 Liberty Drive
Bloomington, IN 47403
www.balboapress.com
844-682-1282

Because of the dynamic nature of the Internet, any web addresses or links contained in this book may have changed since publication and may no longer be valid. The views expressed in this work are solely those of the author and do not necessarily reflect the views of the publisher, and the publisher hereby disclaims any responsibility for them.

Any people depicted in stock imagery provided by Getty Images are models, and such images are being used for illustrative purposes only.
Certain stock imagery © Getty Images.

ISBN: 978-1-6698-2505-0 (sc)
ISBN: 978-1-6698-2506-7 (e)

Print information available on the last page.

Balboa Press rev. date: 02/14/2023

Survivor:

In cancer, a person is considered to be a survivor from the time of diagnosis until the end of life.
https://www.cancer.gov/publications/dictionaries/cancer-terms/def/survivor

> *"Life is like a tree and its root is consciousness. Therefore, once we tend the root, the tree as a whole will be healthy."*
>
> *-Deepak Chopra*

Dedicated to my loved ones who succumbed to cancer, but fought with perseverance till the end…

I chose to use a photograph of trees I took while on a hike in Mammoth Park, Kentucky. For me, a tree represents spirit and strength. Throughout my journey with cancer I'm convinced we have the power to heal ourselves from within. Just as a tree needs nutrients and a healthy environment for its roots, we also need to nourish ours. When I say root I am referring to where the cancer began. To understand why our leaves are dying, we need to understand what is poisoning our roots.

Many heartfelt thank yous to those who have donated to my GoFundMe page at **Hope for Addie Stage IV Metastatic Cancer** *to assist me with treatments and the ability to have this book published.*

CONTENTS

Part 1

ABOUT THIS BOOK

Being told I had stage IV cancer with no cure I lost all hope. I was in disbelief. But then I read the book, *Radical Remission* by Kelly A. Turner, Ph.D. A burst of hopeful light appeared before me. The book is filled with personal stories from victims who have successfully survived since diagnosed many years ago with an incurable cancer. Why didn't my doctor tell me that I too can beat my cancer? Instead I was told I had a year left if I did not follow the chemo protocol he prescribed. While reading Turner's book I became intrigued, empowered. I became curious about my cancer instead of fearful. The day I picked up this book my outlook and life changed completely.

I discovered my purpose in life at the age of 41. I had spent my entire life wondering if I would ever get a sign leading me to my true path. I constantly questioned why I hadn't found it yet and if it would ever arrive.

I believe cancer invaded my body for a reason. Since the second time being diagnosed in my adulthood didn't spark any insight, I strongly feel in the depths of my gut this third diagnosis presented the answer. Surviving a terminal cancer at 13 years old, breast cancer at 37, and the metastasis (spread) of the previous breast cancer to my bones at 41, to me meant I needed to solve this mystery. Like a flash of a light, I then realized I had something to offer: I can share my experiences and victories to help those dealing with cancer.

I realized I had to share what I had endured for more than twenty years. I have hopes for others to feel the vigor of self-trust and self-healing. This was primarily through my awakening to the idea of self-empowerment. I lost control of my own life while I suffered through the first two diagnoses. But that's what happens. The cancer takes over and the fear floods in, leaving you in a world of endless abyss. We stop listening to ourselves and our bodies. And instead, we give away our power.

My intention is to help you retrieve your inner power and to supply you with resources that will lead you on a healing journey.

> *"Yesterday I was clever, so I wanted to change the world. Today I am wise, so I am changing myself."*
>
> —*Rumi*

INTRODUCTION

Knowledge I wish I had while fighting cancer for over two decades

> *"Doctors won't make you healthy. Nutritionists won't make you slim. Teachers won't make you smart. Gurus won't make you calm. Mentors won't make you rich. Trainers won't make you fit. Ultimately, you have to take responsibility. Save yourself."*
>
> *—Naval Ravikant*

I'm a cancer survivor. Cancer struck at 13, 37, and again at 41 years old. I guess you can call me a professional. My first diagnosis was during the Christmas of 1992. A Primitive Neuro Ecto Dermal Tumor (PNET) is what had invaded the left temple of my 13-year-old head. It's a rare cancer that only preys on children and has a 25% survival rate. Somehow, I made it without any recurrence for almost 25 years.

Fast forward to 2016, this time a new cancer: Invasive Ductal Carcinoma, otherwise known as breast cancer. Once again, I went through surgery, radiation, and chemotherapy. I did everything my doctors told me, but nothing my instincts were trying to tell me. I was too weak and tired of living in constant pain. I had no connection with my brain or my heart. I felt lost in a tornado of fear and distress. There were so many questions, but no answers.

At the age of 14 I had no fear. I was invincible as most teenagers believe to be true. As an adult this is not the case. I was confronted with rent, bills, and responsibilities. Trying to keep up with my daily life including a full-time job and countless doctor appointments that were dragging me down. I look back now and I see a person I don't know. Was that really me? A person who could barely walk from one room to another, a person who stopped laughing and smiling, a person who saw no hope in my future? I was lost in that gloomy, spiraling tornado. Yet, I pulled through for the second time, or so I thought.

I had been dealing with severe pain in my left hip for eight months that eventually caused me to rely on a walking cane. I had never experienced pain with my two previous cancers. Each cancer had just popped up in the form of an unwanted lump. Until I received the call for my MRI results, I believed I was just experiencing deep muscle pain. Instead on that Tuesday I was told it was most likely metastatic cancer, and I was scheduled that Friday for an emergency surgery including a biopsy.

The cancer from my breast had returned, but now it had spread to my bones. It was like the cancer was Pac-Man gobbling up my hipbone, leaving fragments of bone to barely hold onto the connecting muscle. That Friday I received an improved leg; a titanium rod was inserted into my left femur bone from the hip down to my knee. I could walk again pain free! Well, somewhat pain free.

The results were in. The physician's assistant entered the room, head down with a somber expression that told me everything I already knew in my heart. The cancer is back. These were scariest words I had ever been told because this time it was Stage IV. There is no Stage V. This is it. This is the end. It felt as if I was living in a black-and-white episode of the *Twilight Zone*.

I was given one year to live if I did not follow the protocol of the oncologist. My option was to be on a full chemotherapy schedule for an indefinite number of years. I had to choose: quality of life or quantity. I could live longer while receiving monthly chemotherapy treatments that are bound to have severe side effects, or I can forgo treatment, but my time would be limited. At first, I chose quality, but now I choose both.

It was instilled in me to believe and trust what the doctor says. But they don't always know what is best for you. You know who does? YOU! This may be the most important lesson I've learned over the years. I've learned to speak up for myself and do what I think is best for my health and my survival. I've learned to listen to other opinions and research. Once I picked up the book *Radical Remission* by Dr. Kelly A. Turner, my life changed. I realized that Stage IV, or any stage of cancer, doesn't have to mean the end. We have choices! We also have hope and tools to continue healing ourselves. This can be seen as 'work', but isn't life worth fighting for?

My approach to healing is through my general oncologist, a naturopathic oncologist, and my own research. Integrative medicine promotes the physical, emotional, and spiritual health of a person by incorporating complementary therapies (physical activity, diet, dietary supplements, mind-body modalities, acupuncture, and massage therapy) with conventional therapy. Throughout this book I will share the methods I have taken to heal with high hopes you can experience a favorable path.

Part 2

PREPARATION & PLANNING

You have been diagnosed with cancer. Now what? Where are you in this challenge? A recent diagnosis? At the halfway point of treatment? Almost done? Maybe it's not your personal journey, but you are a friend, a family member, or a caregiver. Most likely you are dealing with a range of emotions, many of which you have never felt before. It's important to try to accept these feelings and learn how to live with them as best you can. If you have cancer, those feelings may be with you for a long period of time. I hope this book helps you and your loved ones to understand what you are going through.

If you have cancer you may notice every ache, pain, or sign of illness. You may even think about the process of dying. While it's normal to think these thoughts, it's also important to focus on living. It's quite normal to want to hold on to your old life, but you must adapt to survive and feel healthy. Remember that every breath is a gift. Focus on living because death is inevitable.

No two people are alike. Some of this book may apply to your situation and some of it may not. Take from it what interests you and apply it to your new life as a cancer survivor. Every day you conquer is another day you have survived. You are a survivor! You are a warrior, and you must fight to stay as healthy as possible! You are in control of your life. Even though it feels as if your dignity has been stripped away and all control has been lost, it has not.

You can regain some control by choosing what you want. Do you want a doctor that disregards your concerns or ideas to heal? Most likely not. Go get a second opinion, or a third, or even a tenth opinion. Don't settle. The doctor you choose will play a significant role in your healing process. You will have a relationship with your doctor. Do research or have a supportive person to help you. I was so accustomed to doing everything the doctors said because I trusted them. I still trust them now, but it's important to understand that treatment is typically given based upon your type of cancer. Therefore, you are lumped into the statistical treatment plan.

Ask your doctor about being tested to see how medicine and chemotherapy drugs interact with your inherited genes. Pharmacogenomics is a type of genetic testing that shows how inherited genes affect the way medications work for each person (sometimes called pharmacogenetics). [1]

Think about all the ways your body has supported you in the past. Consider the times you've been ill and then recovered, when your body responded well to medical interferences, and the ways your body told you what it needed and how you've responded. You're simply doing that again with your cancer. Your body knows how to heal. We've been taught to search outside ourselves for healing purposes, whether it's drugs or other people's thoughts (including doctors). I think it's time we start looking within ourselves.

Reflect on your inner strengths. Recognize your wisdom, your inner power, and your determination. Learning to live and thrive during your journey, and after, requires you to focus on all the parts of your life: how you act and react, how you think (positive versus negative), how you feel, and *how* you allow yourself to be loved by others and yourself.

I can't stress enough how important it is to have a plan before you embark on this healing journey. I understand it's stressful and it seems easier to throw in the towel and give up. Take some time before making any major choices. Take time to reflect. Even five minutes a day of sitting still with your body and thoughts may help you to choose what is best for yourself.

It's also a perfect time to reach out to family and friends. Most people will want to help you. If they offer, allow them to help you. We need all the love and support we can get during this new life change.

---

[1] https://www.nigms.nih.gov/education/factsheets/Pages/pharmacogenomics.aspx

COMFORTS & CONVENIENCES

Transportation: I thought I would be driving myself to all my treatments, but my father became my private chauffeur. While the side effects may not show until days after your treatment, over time it is quite common that your energy level will diminish. Let's just say that I never had issues walking less than 10 feet from the living room to the kitchen, until after chemotherapy. Nothing compares to the draining effect chemo had. It was as if my life force was being sucked out of each cell like a high-powered vacuum. The suction was consistently depleting my strength both mentally and physically. Having someone to drive me to appointments was crucial.

If you don't have your own personal chauffer, below is a list of companies that will transport you to doctor appointments and to treatments for free.

- 💜 **American Cancer Society**: https://www.cancer.org/treatment/support-programs-and-services/patient-transportation.html
- 💜 **Angel Wheels to Healing**: 8007680238, angelwheels.org Angel Wheels to Healing provides non-emergency, long distance ground transportation to financially disadvantaged patients for treatment.
- 💜 **Good Days:** 877-968-7233, www.mygooddays.org Good Days offers transportation for patients with chronic medicalconditions who have limited financial means.
- 💜 **The SAMFund for Young Adult Survivors of Cancer:** 8664399365, thesamfund.org The SAMFund provides support to young adults who are struggling financially due to cancer. Twice a year, the organization provides grants to survivors aged 21-39 to help with transportation-related expenses, as well as other types of expenses.

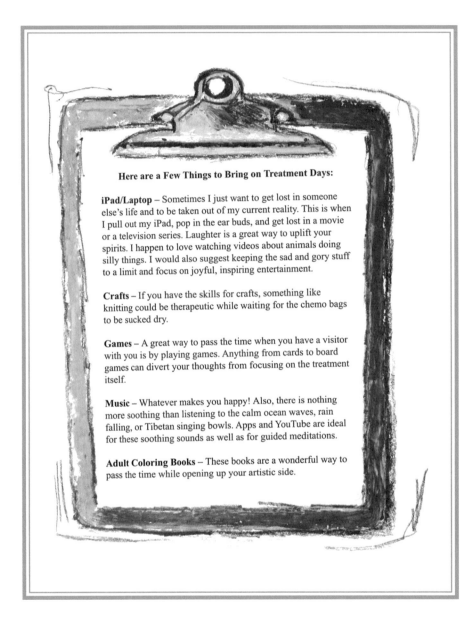

Here are a Few Things to Bring on Treatment Days:

iPad/Laptop – Sometimes I just want to get lost in someone else's life and to be taken out of my current reality. This is when I pull out my iPad, pop in the ear buds, and get lost in a movie or a television series. Laughter is a great way to uplift your spirits. I happen to love watching videos about animals doing silly things. I would also suggest keeping the sad and gory stuff to a limit and focus on joyful, inspiring entertainment.

Crafts – If you have the skills for crafts, something like knitting could be therapeutic while waiting for the chemo bags to be sucked dry.

Games – A great way to pass the time when you have a visitor with you is by playing games. Anything from cards to board games can divert your thoughts from focusing on the treatment itself.

Music – Whatever makes you happy! Also, there is nothing more soothing than listening to the calm ocean waves, rain falling, or Tibetan singing bowls. Apps and YouTube are ideal for these soothing sounds as well as for guided meditations.

Adult Coloring Books – These books are a wonderful way to pass the time while opening up your artistic side.

Finances: Don't let your finances go on life support! Cancer treatment in recent years has come at a steep financial cost. Oncology drugs, doctor bills, hospital bills, lab work, and alternative treatments seem to pile up like a Jenga tower just waiting to crash to the floor.

Solutions:

- 💜 Discuss costs with health care providers as soon as possible. Oral chemo vs. intravenous chemo, doctor fees, hospital charges, and medication costs may or may not be covered even if you have health insurance.
- 💜 Review your insurance policy. Get a summary of your policy that outlines your benefits, any coverage limits, and the appeals process. Find out your deductible and out-of-pocket responsibility.
- 💜 Apply for Grants. Cancer Financial Assistance Coalition https://www.cancerfac.org, CancerCare https://www.cancercare.org, and Cancer.Net https://www.cancer.net
- 💜 Apply for benefits ASAP! It can take a long time for them to process. Social Security https://www.ssa.gov, Medicaid https://www.medicaid.gov Medicare https://www.medicare.gov

- 💜 Keep a journal of all expenses. It can be useful if you need to dispute a charge. It can help you anticipate and prepare for expenses related to your treatment, which will help you to feel less overwhelmed. I like to keep my financial records in an Excel document.
- 💜 Keep copies of medical records, bills, prescription information, health insurance records, and disability insurance records.
- 💜 Ask drug companies for deals. Patient Assistant Programs for free and/or heavily discounted medications – NeedyMeds https://www.needymeds.org
- 💜 Get help with transit and lodging. The American Cancer Society's Road to Recovery and Patient Lodging Programs provide free rides to medical facilities and housing near them. Angel Flight and Air Care Alliance provide free flights to patients in need.
- 💜 Reach out to support groups and social workers. Ask for a social worker on staff at the hospital. CancerCare-Oncology social workers free of charge www.cancercare.org or call 800.813.HOPE (4673)
- 💜 Include your health insurance company in the planning process. Ask to speak with a Case Manager for cost-cutting ideas. To what extent is your treatment plan covered? The Patient Advocate www.patientadvocate.org is a good place to start. Case managers can intervene on your behalf regarding medical debt. They also maintain a network of volunteer attorneys. (Lawhelp.org)
- 💜 Flexible Spending Account (FSA): An FSA account allows you to put pre-tax money from your paycheck into a special account that later can pay for certain medical expenses. This can include co-pays, prescriptions, dental and vision services. It must be set up through an employer.
- 💜 Know your rights regarding your job. The Americans with Disabilities Act & The Family Medical Leave Act often allows cancer patients and their caregivers to take up to 12 weeks of unpaid leave per year.

Job Protection: If you are employed, speak with your Human Resources representative prior to your scheduled treatments. The Family and Medical Leave Act (FMLA) entitles eligible employees of covered employers to take unpaid, job-protected leave for specified family and medical reasons with continuation of group health insurance coverage under the same terms and conditions as if the employee had not taken leave https://www.dol.gov/agencies/whd/fmla. This was critical for me as it protected my employment. I missed countless workdays, and many times I couldn't last more than a couple of hours at the office.

Oral Care: See your dentist prior to beginning any chemotherapy or radiation. This way you will know the status of your current oral health in case an issue arises that wasn't there prior to treatment. There are also some medications such as Biophosphonate and Denosumab that can have a side effect called medication-related osteonecrosis of the jaw (MRONJ), which is bone damage in the jaw. Denosumab reduces the rate of bone remodeling, thereby increasing bone mineral density, improving bone strength, and reducing the risk of fractures.[1]

Any teeth causing problems or needing an extraction now or even possibly in the future should be extracted before starting these drugs. Otherwise, a tooth removal or a dental implant can lead to a lifelong risk even if the Bisphosphonate or Denosumab is stopped. The socket might not heal after a tooth is pulled, bone may be left exposed, or bony fragments may protrude into the mouth, causing sores in the areas that rub up against them. [2] This is rare, but can be a very serious condition. Make sure you thoroughly discuss your medical history with your dentist prior to any dental procedures.

Wig: I fashioned a couple of wigs while I was going through chemo and radiation at the age of 14. The wigs were itchy, hot, and uncomfortable. I've heard major improvements have been made and they are quite fetching now. However, when I was diagnosed again at 38 years old, I wore one about five times

[2] https://www.health.harvard.edu/womens-health/taking-osteoporosis-drugs-shouldnt-prevent-you-from-getting-oral-surgery

and called it quits. I realized I had no shame in having cancer, and I was not embarrassed by the loss of my hair. I gave up the idea that I had to fit in and look "normal." If I must deal with cancer, others can deal with looking at my baldhead, which I was told is nicely shaped. Of course, this is your choice. Some women adorn their head with beautiful silk scarves, hats, or embrace their bareness.

Free wigs can be obtained from these Arizona companies:

- 💜 ***Don't Be a Chump Check for a Lump*** - *provides free breast health education, mammograms, testing, and direct assistance to breast cancer patients* https://www.checkforalump.org/
- 💜 ***Impact One Breast Cancer Foundation*** – https://impactone.pink/
- 💜 ***Reba's Vision*** http://rebasvision.com/basket-of-hope/
- 💜 ***Tina's Treasures Cancer Care Boutique*** – 480-323-1990 https://www.honorhealth.com/medical-services/cancer-care/support-services/tinas-treasures-cancer-care-boutique

Penguin Cap: https://penguincoldcaps.com/
This is a drug free and non-invasive technique of scalp cooling to minimize hair loss. I opted out of this decision because it was a bit pricy for me without insurance. It is possible that your medical insurance company may cover the cost of the cold cap. If your policy covers cranial hair prosthesis, then it may be covered.

Food and Drinks to stock up on prior to treatment:

- 💜 Pedialyte popsicles and drinks
- 💜 Fresh fruit popsicles (no added sugar)
- 💜 Pure coconut water (no added sugar)
- 💜 Veggie broth
- 💜 Rice
- 💜 Quinoa (which is a high protein grain)
- 💜 Nut butter (no added sugar)
- 💜 Plant-based protein powder – I recommend **RAWr! Life Superfoods brand**, which is local, organic, gluten free, vegan, non-GMO, raw, and the best I've ever tried! They ship nationally and internationally. https://www.rawrlife.com/
- 💜 Applesauce (organic, no added sugar)
- 💜 Tea – Green/Chaga/Chamomile
- 💜 Raw Nuts – Walnuts/Cashews/Almonds/Brazil Nuts/Pecans
- 💜 Fresh garlic and ginger

Radiation: What a terrifying word. Radiation. My mind immediately envisions a green glowing light outlining my body as if I was a comic book character. In actuality, there is no pain while receiving treatment; it's the side effects that may occur within a couple weeks you can possibly prevent. Like anything in life there is no guarantee. However, the third time in my life I went through radiation I used the **CamWell** cream after each treatment. I had no physical side effects as previously happened where I ended up with an oozing skin burn that did not heal for many weeks. The ***Herb to Soothe™*** Cream by CamWell is Oncologist-formulated, safe, and non-toxic.[3]

Unfortunately, I had no knowledge of this magical cream four years ago. During that time, my chest was being radiated every day over a month's time. It's the equivalent of being exposed to the sun's rays constantly burning your skin over and over and over. Just imagine the worst sunburn you've ever had. Now imagine that you are required to go stand out in the sun, skin exposed as the rays continue to burn deeper and deeper until your skin is incapable of healing. The open wound seeps, cracks, and cries out for an end to the torture. I'm not saying this will happen to you, but be prepared for the worst and definitely order this amazing cream! If you do happen to experience severe burning, ask your Radiologist about Lidocaine frosting. This pure white, thick cream will add a numbing and cooling sensation when applied directly to the burn site.

Wear loose fitting clothes to get in and out of that aren't constricting near the radiated area. This will save time and effort while at the clinic as you will most likely have to change into a gown each time.

Radiation is usually done every weekday anywhere from weeks to months. If you need transportation, please see the Preparation section in the beginning of the book. The good thing is that the radiation appointments generally only last from 10 to 30 minutes including the office waiting time.

---

[3] https://ourcamwell.com/shop-our-products/oncology-skin-care-for-radiation-therapy-patients/

Part 3

DURING TREATMENT

"The secret of health for both mind and body is not to mourn for the past, not to worry about the future, not to anticipate troubles, but to live in the present moment wisely and earnestly."

—Buddha

If I had to describe a typical treatment environment, I would say that it feels like being in an exclusive hospital. Everyone has their own reclining chair, a heated blanket, and walls adorned with photographic images of soothing nature scenes. The last clinic I visited even had a private room where you could dim the lights and drift away while napping on a plush couch.

I suggest you bring additional blankets and a cozy pillow. For me this was, and is, a must! The Infusion room felt like a meat locker, and I was the frozen slab of meat. The chill from the air would sweep over my skin until my entire body was covered in goose bumps. There was nothing worse than having every inch of my body go into a frantic shiver. To take it up a notch, gloves and a comfy hat can also help to ease you into a state of comforting tranquility by staying warm.

While this sounds contradictory, wearing very cold socks and gloves during chemo may help to eliminate neuropathy. Neuropathy is damage or dysfunction of one or more nerves that typically results in numbness, tingling, muscle weakness and pain in the affected area. Wet socks and gloves then place them in the freezer for a few minutes. I would bring a small cooler to treatment to store my socks and gloves until I was ready for the infusion. Wear the socks and gloves for as long as you can endure the cold during the infusion.

There are some herbs and spices that may help protect your nerve cells from damage such as spirulina, ginger, and flax seeds, which can be ground up and added to smoothies, dairy free yogurt, and oatmeal. Curcumin is the main ingredient of curcuma longa, and has a variety of effects, such as anti-oxidative, anti-inflammatory, immunomodulatory, and neuro-protective.[4]

Something else that may help is alpha-lipoic acid as it is an antioxidant said to lower blood sugar levels, improve nerve function, and relieve uncomfortable and painful symptoms in the legs and arms. Massaging the afflicted areas with lotion may also help alleviate the pain. Some lotions to try are those that contain cocoa butter or menthol.

---

[4] https://www.ncbi.nlm.nih.gov/pmc/articles/PMC3946321/

> *Physical activity can reduce death from breast cancer by about 40% in early-stage patients. It has the most powerful effect of any lifestyle factor."*
>
> *–Dr. Julie Gralow, Fred Hutch / SCCA / UW physician-scientist*

Exercise is another approach that can increase blood flow to the hands and feet and may offer temporary relief from pain as well. If you have the energy, you can try to do a brisk walk for about 20 minutes. If your clinic has the space, you may even try walking during your treatment. Some clinics have begun implementing exercise during the infusions as the results have shown vast improvement in healing. Exercise to help flush out toxins as it causes changes to antibodies, releases endorphins, and slows the release of stress hormones. [5]

Exercise appears to be an effective adjunct therapy through multiple studies. According to Harvard Medical School, in one analysis of 61 clinical trials of women with all stages of breast cancer, those who underwent an exercise program during treatment had significantly improved quality of life, fitness, energy, and strength, as well as significantly less anxiety, depression, and a lower body mass index and waist circumference compared with the regular care groups. [6]

Wearing something for easy access to your Power Port or your arm for the intravenous infusions is also necessary. I learned the hard way when I put myself in contorted positions flailing around like an octopus, arms searching for an escape from my turtleneck sweater. I wonder if the patients around me were wondering if I was attempting some sort of a strip tease. Eventually I was able to free myself from the constricting turtleneck to expose my port. Victory!

The following are strategies to help minimize the toxicity of chemotherapy drugs that we are not always told about. The following strategies were recommended by my Naturopathic Oncologist while I was

---

[5] https://www.health.harvard.edu/staying-healthy/excercising-to-relax
[6] https://www.health.harvard.edu/blog/exercise-as-part-of-cancer-treatment-2018061314035

getting infusions of *Carboplatin, Taxotere, Herceptin,* and *Perjeta.* Talk with your Naturopath provider to see if the following will also aid you in preventing negative side effects from the drugs you are prescribed.

- 💜 If you are receiving *Taxotere,* or another chemo drug that can cause nerve damage, follow this protocol: Wet and then freeze a couple pairs of cotton gloves and cotton socks. You can keep them in a small cooler that you bring to treatment. Wear both the socks and gloves during the drug infusion. Basically, the cold reduces capillary circulation in your hands and feet. Because of this, the accumulation of chemo is reduced and thus reduces nerve damage.
- 💜 Chew on ice and drink only cold drinks during your infusion to help prevent mouth sores.
- 💜 Movement is critical! Take walking laps (as you are able) in the infusion center. Any type of movement increases the effectiveness of chemotherapy as stated previously.
- 💜 Paint your nails with dark opaque nail polish to preserve nail health during the Taxotere therapy. Before bed each night, rubbing Jojoba oil onto your nail beds may also help.
- 💜 To help reduce bacteria in your mouth and throat keep a jar of salty water in your kitchen and bathroom. Swish, gargle, and spit this water as many times a day as you can tolerate. This will reduce the development of mouth sores.

In preparation for chemo day, a 24-hour fasting before the start of your infusion can reduce side effects. Fasting will aid cell death by highly stressing out the malignant cells. According to Dr. Lise Alschuler, a naturopathic oncologist and cancer survivor, it is recommended to continue the fast the day of treatment and then the following day. The good news is you can consume water, coconut water, and vegetable broths during the fasting period. If needed, you can eat low carb vegetables as a soup, cooked, raw, or juiced. If you need further food/energy you can also have two tablespoons of coconut oil and unsweetened coconut milk. If you become too weak or dizzy from the fast, consume boiled eggs and soaked nuts.

- 💜 **Finger Band-Aids** – (As referred to on page 19) Use these if you experience your fingernails or toenails start to wiggle and become loose. It's best to keep them bandaged. Although it's quite frustrating to continually reapply the Band-Aids once they become wet and/or old, it's much better than having them accidentally ripped off.
- 💜 **Hydration/Pedialyte** – This was a lifesaver for me! Instead of Gatorade, I opted for something with low sugar. If you encounter endless days of diarrhea and find yourself dehydrated, this drink or popsicles with save the day! I would also suggest asking your nurse for hydrating fluids via IV during treatment.

- 💜 **Fruit popsicles** – There is something about cold, refreshing popsicles when everything else tastes terrible and is difficult to ingest. Again, I would opt for low sugar, natural popsicles. You can also make your own with pureed fruit mixes with a natural sweetener such as agave, monk fruit, or honey.
- 💜 **Healthy Weight Gain shake** – (See recipe in Part 5) Sip on this during your day through a straw. I love my metal straw that can be used over and over. This way you cut down on useless trash and help the marine environment too! By utilizing the straw, it enables you to bypass the taste buds on your tongue. Then your belly is full and happy with no need to worry about a terrible taste.
- 💜 **Soft, warm blanket & Socks** – For me this was a must! It's better to be over-prepared as in most treatment rooms I've been in are quite cold.
- 💜 **Positive mind** – Meditation was a scary word until I learned what it really entailed. I found myself waking up in the morning already in mid-thought asking myself silly questions like, "What time should I go to the gym? What body part do I work out? Wait. Is today my day off from the gym? What do I wear to dinner Saturday night?" Arg! Be quiet, brain! I envisioned that I would wake up with a perfectly clear head. Boy was I wrong! I spent time at the Cancer Support Community in Phoenix attending free healing classes, including: Sound Meditation, Tibetan Singing Bowl Meditation, and Mindful Meditation. I was amazed to learn how 10 minutes a day, or even five minutes, is all it takes. And the best part is that the point is quite the opposite of clearing your mind. Being mindful is bringing yourself and your thoughts into the present, focusing on emotions, thoughts, and sensations that you're experiencing "in the now".[7] Visit Cancer Support Communities website for a mediation schedule at: https://www.cancersupportcommunity.org/
- 💜 **Journal** – Keep a daily log of any side effects you experience. Note the date and time, and measure how they affect you on a scale from one to 10 including what relief method worked if any. You can also keep track of your finances. For example, you can make a list of payments made and owed. This is a wonderful way to keep track of your progress and to see trends in your medical journey.
- 💜 **Music** – We've all heard how the rhythm and melody of music can be a form of healing. Here are a few of my favorite outlets for listening pleasure found on YouTube: templesounds, SleepTube, Meditative Mind, and Hay House.

---

[7] https://www.fammed.wisc.edu/mindfulness/research/

Also, here are specific songs I find peace with which are listed below:

Biomes – James Heather
Opus 23 – Dustin O'Halloran
Gaze – *Moux*
Zaouiat Ahansal – Pablo Nouvelle
Ascent – Ludovico Einaudi
Symmetry (Piano Solo) – SYML
Luna From Soyuz Tomasz Krall
Escape from Gravity – Deuter
Heart Chakra – Beautiful Chorus
A Distant Light – Marconi Union
Weightless – Marconi Union
Ya Devi (Deep Relaxation) – Edo & Jo
Gho Mata (Unconditional Love) – Edo & Jo
Finding a Place – Trent Reznor and Atticus Ross
Nuvole bianche – Ludovico Einaudi
Watermark – Enya
Liberi – Zibra Inguzu
Prad – Yann Tiersen
Seven Days Walking/Day 2: Birdsong - Ludovico Einaudi

💜 **Essential Oils & Aromatherapy** – There are many benefits to using oils. They can assist with physical pain, boost wellbeing, relieve stress and anxiety, and enhance meditation and spirituality. [8] Regarding issues with nausea, three essential oils that can help are peppermint, ginger, and lavender. Please contact Karen Janusz for additional information or to schedule an appointment at 602.882.2976.
Karen.janusz@kjholistic.com, www.myyl.com/kjanusz,
www.kjholistic.com

💜 Cannabinoids: The use of cannabinoids containing plant extracts as herbal medicine can be traced back to as early as 500 BC. (Footnote - https://doi.org/10.3390/cancers12113203) We are now learning so much more about the benefits in regard to our mental and physical health. Without the use of medical CBD (non intoxicating) and THC (triggers the brain to release

---

[8] https://www.hopkinsmedicine.org/health/wellness-and-prevention/aromatherapy-do-essential-oils-really-work

dopamine "feel good" chemical) I would not be able to eat and be as pain free as I have been. It has increased my appetite, lessened my nausea, and reduced my body pains. Along with these benefits, the use of CBD and THC have also helped with feelings of anxiety and depression. In addition to THC, CBD is another plant-derived cannabinoid that has been extensively studied for its potential antitumor effects.[9] I prefer to take it in the tincture form without any added flavoring. There are so many other forms of ingestion that can be utilized as well. Check out your local dispensaries for more information. One I specifically prefer is SOL Flower. Jane Fix is the Director of Patient Services and is available for free consultations.[10]

My naturopathic oncologist set me up with a heavy-duty number of supplements during treatment to continue ensuring my body was in constant healing mode. Everyone is unique even though you may have the same diagnosis as others. Therefore, I would recommend talking with a naturopathic doctor or an oncology nutritionist before implementing any supplements into your plan.

This list of supplements is what I was prescribed by my naturopath doctor, Dr. Lise Alschuler, and some I chose for myself through extensive research. The protocol changes overtime so be aware that supplements can work in the beginning but may end up being replaced with another. Also, these supplements are recommended based on the individual and treatment. Please contact your doctor before adding any supplements to your daily regimen.

- 🖤 **American Ginseng** – Reduces fatigue and optimizes our stress response system (hypothalamic, pituitary, adrenal axis). It has been clinically demonstrated to specifically reduce fatigue associated with chemotherapy. [11]
- 🖤 **Astragalus** – Protection for the kidneys. Enhances immune function. Reduces nausea. [12]
- 🖤 **Bioplasma cell salts** – Maintains electrolyte balance, reduces nausea, improves appetite, reduces diarrhea, and lessens fatigue.[13]

---

9 https://ncbi.nlm.nih.gov/pmc/articles/PMC6387667/ Cannabinoids in cancer treatment: Therapeutic potential and legislation (nih.gov)

10 https://www.livewithsol.com/ Medical and Recreational Cannabis Dispensaries - Sol Flower (livewithsol.com)

11 https://www.mayo.edu/research/forefront/ginseng-fights-fatigue-cancer-patients

12 https://www.mskcc.org/cancer-care/integrative-medicine/herbs/astragalus

13 https://www.emersonecologics.com/blog/post/cancer-survive-ithrive-the-path-to-health-after-cancer-treatment

- 💜 **Curcumin** – Anti-tumor properties. Plays a preventative role in the development of cancer. Fortifies healthy cells. [14]
- 💜 **Enhanced Zinc lozenges** – Helps your immune system and metabolism function and is also important to wound healing and your sense of taste and smell per Dr. Lise Alschuler, ND, FABNO.
- 💜 **Glutamine Powder** – 10 grams, two to three times daily, for ceasing diarrhea because of it's anti-inflammatory effects. [15]
- 💜 **Maitake** – Extracts are more powerful anticancer and immune-enhancing agents than any of the other medicinal mushrooms![16]
- 💜 **Melatonin** – Increases overall survival, reduces chemo-associated toxicities, and provides immune support. Meditation also produces high levels of melatonin. The more you meditate, the more virus antibodies you produce.[17]
- 💜 **ProThrivers Wellness Brain** – Supports brain function, increases Nerve Growth Factor, which increases new neuron development and new neuronal connections (neuroplasticity). This specifically is targeted to support brain function to counteract "chemo brain," per Dr. Lise Alschuler, ND, FABNO
- 💜 **RF Plus by Integrative Therapeutics** – Two capsules, two times daily for ceasing diarrhea.
- 💜 **Vitamin D Plus K** – Beneficial for bone and cardiovascular health.[18]

[14] https://www.ncbi.nlm.nih.gov/pmc/articles/PMC6835707/

[15] https://badgut.org/information-centre/health-nutrition/glutamine/

[16] https://www.liebertpub.com/doi/abs/10.1089/jmf.2012.0222

[17] https://www.sciencedirect.com/science/article/abs/pii/0306987795902996

[18] https://www.ncbi.nlm.nih.gov/pmc/articles/PMC5613455/

Part 4

POSITIVE TRANSITION

"There is one consolation in being sick; and that is the possibility that you may recover to a better state than you were ever in before."

–Henry David Thoreau

Have you dreamt of lying on a cloud-like pillow while being fed juicy grapes following a soothing massage, a personal chef whipping up a feast fit for the Gods, just for you? We can't make such fantasies a reality (and perhaps shouldn't), but we can get close. Although I have not been hand-fed grapes, I have accepted help from those who offer any assistance to help me feel at ease. As much as I wanted people to help me out, this was the most difficult thing to ask for. It was one thing if family and friends just did helpful things for me, but to ask, well I just couldn't do it. I already felt like a burden. Eventually I realized that when people offer their support: LET THEM! They want to help you.

If family or friends offer to cook for you, let them. It's hard not to be able to do the simple things you were so accustomed to do so easily in the past. I wish I would've asked for more help the second time I was diagnosed. Most people don't know what to do for someone dealing with cancer. They will say something like, "Please let me know if there is anything I can do to help." However, this is a very open-ended statement.

While going through the life-changing events and all the dynamics it entails, the last thing I could do is tell people what I really needed. That question puts me in a state of frantic confusion. I begin to wonder what I could ask for that is not too outlandish. It's like being a manager and delegating tasks to employees. But I don't want to be a manager; I just want people to do things with no questions asked. Better yet, they can offer something specific and then ask if that is something that will be beneficial for you. If you are comfortable asking, it can be easier on them instead leaving them in a state of wonder. It then becomes easy for you as well because you get what you know will help you the most and make you feel better.

> *When someone gives you a gift, take it as a gift. Allow it to lighten your load. If you need to immediately switch to "Oh my God, I have to repay them," you've turned their gift into a burden."*
>
> *–Anita Moorjani*

For those who are not going through life with cancer, the best thing you could do to help is to just do something, anything. It was even more difficult when people said, "Just let me know what I can do to help." It doesn't sound like it would be complicated to give a response, but with everything else going on that makes a cancer patient's life chaotic; the last thing we need is to make more decisions. Our life becomes nothing more but decisions day after day. Constant doctor appointments, medical scans, blood count tests, anxiety, depression, and the list goes on.

For example, a dear friend sent me three days of delicious, healthy prepared meals. *Urban Remedy* makes incredibly raw, tasty meals, desserts, juices and smoothies that can be delivered right to your front door. Recently *Whole Foods* started carrying this brand, and I highly recommend trying all they have to offer. Don't let the price scare you. Another dear friend would randomly send me gift cards for grocery stores, which really helped financially.

On that note, for those who know someone going through a cancer journey here are some tips that would certainly be helpful:

- ♥ Just call to let them know you are thinking about them
- ♥ Bring healthy meals, beverages, snacks, but first verify what foods they are/aren't eating
- ♥ Offer to run errands and help with chores, e.g. clean the home,
- ♥ walk their dog, do the laundry, etc.
- ♥ Plan a pampering day - spa day at home or out at a salon/wellness center
- ♥ Anything else you may think will boost the spirits of the person

Post-Treatment Healing Methods

Keep active! – This is one of the key factors to healing. Just simple stretching while sitting or standing still gets the blood flowing to your muscles. Other forms of exercise include yoga, walking (even if it's only from room to room in your house, you're still moving), light housework, etc.

Survivorship care plan – Create a checklist that includes your state of health at the end of treatment, future schedule of visits, who will deliver follow-up care, tests that will be done and why, what long-term effects may occur, symptoms to watch for that might signal a return of your cancer or a new cancer, a list of habits that can interfere with your recovery, and the steps to take to adopt a healthier lifestyle.

Cancer Support Community Center – It's totally free! This non-profit organization began in 1999, to provide support and free classes *So That No One Faces Cancer Alone®*. Some examples of the community classes they provide at no cost for cancer patients and their family and friends are Mindful Meditation, Sound Meditation, Grief & Loss, Hypnotherapy, a variety of art activities, support groups, and many more. Check for your local community support center toll-free at 1.888.793.9355. For Arizona residents visit this website for further information: https://cscaz.org/

The "new normal" life – The realization is that after diagnosis and treatment your "normal life" never really goes back to what it was before cancer. It can take time to adapt to your "new normal," and it can bring up lots of emotions. Be kind to yourself and consider counseling or a support group to help process these emotions. Part of the Cancer Support Community listed above is MyLifeLine. Through this website you can document your journey, create your own private website, and join discussion boards which are available 24/7. If you've been given the clear from cancer and your doctor tells you to go back to your old ways of eating, drinking alcohol, etc... well it's just not practical. We have to adapt to our "new normal," or as I prefer to call it, "the natural state." We must continue our healing process with minimal disruption. Avoiding unhealthy, carcinogenic foods and increasing physical activity along with meditation can lead to a cancer free future. https://mylifeline.org

Reduce inflammation – High levels of inflammation can disrupt the function of the immune system allowing cancer to manifest.[19] It is critical to continue healing yourself with nutritious foods not only during treatment, but as a life-long principle. The focus on maintaining this lifestyle will assist in keeping the cancer from returning. Consume foods that contain probiotics (e.g. fermented foods). Prebiotic Fiber enhances the growth and metabolism of the probiotic bacteria in the gut. Supplements containing acacia gum and baobab fruit derivatives are a terrific source for fiber. Polyphenols are antioxidants that help reduce inflammation too.[20] Eating apples, berries, broccoli, spinach, black beans, almonds, flax seeds, cinnamon, dark chocolate, olives, and olive oil contain these polyphenols. [21]

Sleep – Sleep is critical for your health. Lack of restorative sleep directly enhances inflammation, which can aggravate the cancer. Here are some tips from Dr. Lise Alschuler, ND, FABNO: Eat protein with dinner. Protein will help to stabilize blood sugar overnight and prevent blood sugar drops from causing wakefulness. Stop ingesting caffeine after 2pm, minimize screen time in the evening as the blue light from computers, tablets, phones, and TV can inhibit the hormone Melatonin and make it more difficult to fall asleep. Make your bedroom as dark as possible. Using an eye mask will also help. Keep your

---

19 https://www.ncbi.nlm.nih.gov/pmc/articles/PMC2866629/
20 https://www.drperlmutter.com/reducing-inflammation-for-better-health/
21 https://www.healthline.com/nutrition/polyphenols

bedroom cool as being too warm prevents deep sleep. Develop a pre-sleep routine for relaxation. Things like mediation, deep breathing, and gentle stretching can all help reduce brain arousal.

Lower stress – Easier said than done, but it's possible. From reading *Radical Remission,* I learned the **FEAR** acronym meaning. **F**alse **E**vidence **A**ppearing **R**eal. We are not healing ourselves when fear is present as the immune system shuts down. We delve into the Fight-or-Flight mode instead of the Rest-and-Repair mode, which our body needs to fight off the cancer. Where does your stress come from? Are you creating it by feeding it with negative thoughts? Sometimes we must be vulnerable and dig deeper to get to the root cause. It's possible you can make small or big changes to release stressors from your life. But remember to also give yourself a break. In other words, don't beat yourself up! Forgiveness when goals aren't reached is key. I used to give myself goals for each day, but they were unrealistic and unachievable. I learned to stop putting so much pressure on myself and to remind myself that I am still a strong person even if I couldn't complete all my daily tasks. Learn to create easier goals for yourself rather than beating yourself up for goals you may not be able to meet. Our lives have taken a turn, a shift in a direction created by dealing with cancer. Therefore, learning to create easier goals that you can achieve makes them more achievable.

Mindfulness/Meditation – It is impossible to make your thoughts completely disappear. Paying attention on purpose and without judgment is the definition of Mindful Meditation. Instead of trying to make your mind shut down, concentrate on your body to tie wandering thoughts back to your breath and body. Stress stems from increased production of the "stress" hormone cortisol. Cortisol then acts directly on the gut wall to increase permeability, which enhances the production of inflammatory chemicals throughout the body.[22] Meditation has shown to lower cortisol, reduce inflammation, balance the immune system, and even improve empathy and compassion when done for as little as 10 minutes a day.[23]

Gratitude journal – By putting this into practice, you will soon realize there are many things to be grateful for even when it doesn't feel that way. I have a small journal that is solely dedicated to what I am grateful for each day. (I have even written that I am grateful for having cozy pillows!) It can be anything big or small. Another great thing about this is that once you begin this journal, you may notice little bits of gratitude all around you. You may become more aware and with that your healing process may even be felt throughout your body. Doing this everyday only takes a few minutes, and soon you will realize there is an abundance to be grateful for even if it's as simple as a drop of rain.

---

[22] https://www.ncbi.nlm.nih.gov/pmc/articles/PMC5794709/
[23] https://hr.harvard.edu/files/humanresources/files/mindfulness_now_and_zen.pdf

Release emotions – Practice daily forgiveness. Make a thought journal where you write down all the emotions you felt in a day, then write down what you were thinking just before you felt the way you did. This helps to determine why we felt that specific emotion. It will help you discover the contributing feelings.

Take a Stress Management course for Mindfulness-Based Stress Reduction (MBSR). Emotions should flow through the body like a waterfall. Try hypnosis or Eye Movement Desensitization and Reprocessing EMDR (check your insurance plan for coverage). Eye Movement Desensitization and Reprocessing (EMDR) therapy is an extensively researched, effective psychotherapy method proven to help people recover from trauma and other distressing life experiences, including PTSD, anxiety, depression, and panic disorders. [24] EMDR helps heal trauma and life events that continue to impact a person's psyche resulting in distress. It loosens up the memory networks of the brain using eye movements so that information that was once stuck can find its own resolve and become stored adaptively.

Leave positive notes around the house, at work, in the car, anywhere: *Today is going to be a fantastic day! This is a brand-new day!* Even if you don't believe this, by seeing and reading these words our brain can be "tricked" to believe it's true. Start your days with a smile.

Vision boards – Creativity is also another healing outlet. This project can be catered to however you like. I have made several vision boards: Career, Home, Healing, and a general board of magazine clippings. These images brought and continue to bring me joy and hope for the future. Many years ago, I had made a board with images of Italy, specifically the Liguria area. When I returned from living in Italy, I found my vision board in my storage, and it was full of images of places I had lived near and visited frequently. I created that future without even knowing!

ME time! – Make time for yourself: bath time, art, nature, walk, pampering, cry, write, schedule a massage, Reiki, acupressure, acupuncture, aromatherapy, etc... Of course these suggestions are based on my experience and what I feel works for me. Find what benefits you. I always give something a chance. If then I don't feel it's for me, I move on and try another approach. Then again we don't always have the ability to witness the transformation of our heath from the outside. For example, it may take more than a couple sessions of these therapies for the results to show. Allow yourself to discover the potential of alternative therapies.

---

[24] https://www.emdria.org/about-emdr-therapy/

Baby Steps! – It took me over 20 years to realize that not everything has to be done in one day. Things can wait. Your health and well-being can't. Any approach to making your life as easy as possible, but still rewarding, can make a significant impact on your healing journey.

Socialize – Don't isolate yourself! Even though you may feel you are alone, I promise that you are not. We are all going through our own journey, but those also facing cancer can understand our emotions. The Cancer Support Community I've referenced earlier in the book has helped me significantly. I've met some incredible people who I feel a connection with.

Consider starting a blog to share your journey so you don't have to constantly answer to everyone by reiterating your progress. MyLifeLine.org as stated earlier is a web resource to help you keep friends and family updated and to receive messages in an efficient way.

Toenails – Once the nails on my two big toes fell off, I invested in packages of fake toenails. At least this way I didn't have to subject the world to my troll toes. I wouldn't recommend applying anything to your fingernails or toenails until you've finished treatment, and you've been cleared from having a fungal infection. I waited months until I applied the toenails as my toes were still sensitive to the touch, and I didn't have enough regrowth for the fake nails to attach to anything. I would also like to emphasize that you should not use these if your toenails become thick, discolored, and/ or painful. If you notice any of these symptoms tell your doctor immediately. This may be a fungal infection called *Onychomycosis*. This is most likely from the chemotherapy as it suppresses your immune system, leaving you susceptible to this and other infections. You may also notice that your nails lift from the nail bed, split or crumble, or look scaly. In the meantime, clean your nails with soap and water daily. If your nails are thick and rough, use a urea cream (Aluvea, Keralac) to soften and then wrap your feet in bandages at night. Afterwards wash off the cream, clip your nails, and file them. You can then use an over-the-counter fungal treatment once the nails are cleaned and trimmed. A few other treatments include applying Vicks VapoRub, snakeroot extract, or tea tree oil to the affected nails each day.[25] Be patient as it may take up to 18 months for your nails to grow back fully and be healthy.

Hair re-growth – I like to use natural products to help speed along the growth of hair, eyelashes, and eyebrows. There are clinics that specialize in hair loss, but can be quite expensive. I use the following concoction: in a small jar mix equal parts of castor oil, vitamin E, and essential oils like peppermint and/ or rosemary. The peppermint is quite pungent, so I wouldn't recommend this on the eyelashes as it can

---

[25] https://www.healthline.com/health/home-remedies-for-toenail-fungus

cause a mild stinging in the eyes. On the scalp it's quite invigorating and leaves a tingling sensation. That sensation is what is helping your scalp to come alive.

Unfortunately, my eyebrows never grew back after I finished my chemo treatments. Drawing them in every morning only to have sweat drip down my face to create a 90's flashback of the Vanilla Ice rapper's eyebrow slits wasn't functional. Micro-*blading* is a technique using a super-fine pen made of 12 to 15 needles to deposit pigment into skin. If you are in Arizona I highly recommend *Jessica Pink* who does phenomenal work making the eyebrows look incredibly natural. Since I visited her in 2019, I continue to get compliments. [26]

Vitamin C buffered (capsules) – This is a powerful antioxidant that protects against infection and enhances immunity. It increases production of white blood cells and antibodies. If you have a sensitive stomach and are prone to diarrhea, make sure you take the "buffered" Vitamin C.[27] It can be found in citrus fruit, strawberries, papaya, kiwi, broccoli, red pepper, and brussel sprouts.

Probiotics – These fight pathogenic infections and promote recovery from infections by stimulating the production of antibodies. Probiotics can improve the behavior of the immune system.[28]

Zinc – This is the most important immune mineral as it helps prevent a weakened immune system. You can get your Zinc intake from nuts, seeds, and legumes with oysters ranking as containing the most zinc.[29]

Omega-3 fatty acids – These lipids are essential immune boosters. They help increase phagocytes, the white blood cells that eat up bacteria. They also help to strengthen cell membranes – since your cell membranes (which are like walls to keep all the parts in) are made of these! – to speed up healing and strengthen resistance to infection.[30]

---

[26] 7310 E 6th Avenue Scottsdale, AZ 81 602.358.9387
[27] https://www.iherb.com/blog/buffered-vs-unbuffered-vitamin-c-what-are-the-benefits/620
[28] https://www.karger.com/Article/FullText/496426
[29] https://ods.od.nih.gov/factsheets/Zinc-HealthProfessional/
[30] https://www.ncbi.nlm.nih.gov/pmc/articles/PMC6834330/

Echinacea – These support and strengthen immune system. Echinacea stimulates the white blood cells and lymph cells to attack viruses and bacteria. Look for the species *E.pururea* that guarantees high levels of all three active ingredients: alkylamides, polysaccharides, and chicoric acid.[31]

Allow your body to let you know what it needs, and trust that it will tell you. Sit in silence. Don't rush into decisions. Explore alternative treatments and ideas. Get a second, third, and fourth opinion until you feel confident about what to do. Do whatever it takes until you feel respected as a patient and most of all as a person. This is your life, your body, and ultimately, your decisions.

> *"One day you will tell your story of how you overcame what you went through, and it will be someone else's survival guide."*
>
> *–Brene Brown*

---

[31] https://womensvoice.com/en-us/articles/health/the-rise-and-fall-of-antibiotics/

Part 5

NUTRITION

"One should eat to live, not live to eat."
—Hippocrates

> *"The food you eat can be either the safest and most powerful form of medicine or the slowest form of poison."*
>
> —*Ann Wigmore*

Please get rid of as much sugar from your diet as possible. Even though sugar feeds cancer, cancer will find and use multiple sources for fuel.[32] These days it seems almost impossible to eliminate sugar, and while you think you may be choosing the healthier option, look again. Sugar is added unnecessarily to foods such as ketchup, salad dressings, juice, pizza, breads, yogurt, pasta, soups, etc. The list could go on forever!

An affordable alternative to purchasing groceries can be done through *Imperfect Foods*. They provide sustainable, affordable groceries that can be delivered to your door on a weekly basis. By signing up with a grocery plan you can shop from home. The rejected products from grocery stores are perfectly good that would otherwise go to waste. Discontinued products, surplus, imperfection, and ends and pieces are the main reasons these products are offered through *Imperfect Foods* to the public. https://imperfectfoods.com

Here is a list of products I like to consistently have in the house:

- 💜 **Prepared Meals** – My favorite prepared line of nutritious food called *Urban Remedy* can be found at Whole Foods. Vegan, Gluten-free, Organic, Non-GMO pure food. By far this is the best all around packaged, insanely delicious prepared food I have ever had. However, if you are being cautious of your sodium intake I would avoid or limit any prepackaged foods as they tend to have high amounts of sodium.
- 💜 **Coconut water** – Flavored or plain and buy the ones without added sugar.
- 💜 **Vegan Jell-O/Pudding**
- 💜 **Fruit popsicles** – As referenced in Part 2
- 💜 **Soup** – This can be a very comforting food source. The wonderful thing about soup is that you can make it as chunky or liquefied as you like and be able to freeze it in large amounts.

---

[32] https://cancersecrets.com/cancer-loves-sugar/

I find it to be a simple and satisfying nutritional source. You can just add a bag of dried beans to a Crock Pot with veggie broth and any other veggies you like. There is something about the warmth traveling from your mouth down your esophagus and then into your belly that soothes.

Also, you can choose warm or cold soups depending on how the temperature affects your current state. Sometimes food that is too cold or too hot can increase a side effect you may be having. Make sure to listen to your body for what makes it happiest.

The recipes below were provided from my previous Naturopathic Oncologist, Dr. Lise Alschuler ND, FABNO. https://www.drlise.net/

White Rice Congee	Vegan Avocado Chocolate Mousse	Healthy Weight Gain Shake
A soothing, low residue porridge that is easy to digest and avoids intestinal irritation. You can make this either sweet or savory. ¾ cup white rice 9 cups water *Sweet* – Maple syrup (plant-based sugar), cinnamon, cardamom *Savory* – Italian or curry spices Bring the rice to a boil in the water. Turn the heat down to medium low, cover and let simmer for one hour to get the consistency of porridge. Add your desired seasonings or spices.	This will help to increase calories and healthy fats. 1 large, ripe avocado ¼ cup raw cocoa powder ¼ cup plant-based milk 2 tsp natural sweetener 1 tsp natural vanilla extract *Optional extras*: toasted sliced almonds, chia seeds, frozen mixed berries, almond butter, cocoa nibs, coconut oil Puree the avocado until smooth. Mix the cocoa powder and milk until combined and add to the avocado. Stir in the sweetener, vanilla extract, and any extra ingredients and mix well. Transfer the mousse to individual bowls and store in the fridge until ready to eat. Yum!	550 calories (approx. 65% fat, 25% protein, 10% carbohydrate) 1 cup frozen mixed berries 1 tbsp almond butter ¼ avocado ½ tsp extra-virgin coconut butter 1 tbsp pumpkin seeds 1 tbsp hemp seeds or substitute 1 tbsp high quality omega-3 fat (flax or fish oil) 2 walnuts ½ cup unsweetened almond milk ½ cup water 1 small scoop green powder (spirulina, barely grass, or other greens powder) [from Mark Hyman's book, 10-Day Detox Diet-with adaptations added] Drink through a straw to bypass your taste buds if having nausea.

*If you or someone can juice raw vegetables and fruits on a daily basis, take advantage of this. Juicing gives your body pure nutrients. Remember to drink them immediately or within 24 hours and stored in glass jars with a lid. Besides, it's almost impossible to eat as many fruits and veggies as what a juicing machine can produce.

A few of my favorite juice recipes are as follows:

- 💜 **Green Machine** – One head of romaine, four pieces of kale or two handfuls of spinach, four celery sticks, one lemon, one inch of fresh ginger, and two green apples. Of course, you can always experiment and alter this to your liking. Limes and pineapple are also tasty in this juice.
- 💜 **Orange Juice** – Juice six carrots, one golden beet, one large orange and fresh Turmeric. You may add pineapple, apples, and ginger.
- 💜 **Celery** – Yup, just straight up celery juice. It's not as terrible as it sounds. Sometimes it can even be a bit sweet! I recommend drinking it daily. Celery juice is highly beneficial as it feeds the good bacteria in your gut and boosts your immune system. In multiple studies it has shown to help fight cancer and reduce inflammation, which contributes to many illnesses.[33]

> *"Cancer is not a disease of our genes, it is a disease of what we are feeding them."*
> – Dr. Nasha Winters, ND, L.Ac., FABNO

Foods and additives to AVOID:

- 💜 **Sodium Nitrate** – Sodium nitrate and sodium nitrite are used as preservative agents in cured meats, such as bacon, sausage, and ham, and in some cheeses.[34]
- 💜 **Sugar** – Cancer ingests sugar faster than healthy cells, which causes cancer to grow and spread. According to researchers from Harvard Medical School, it was reported that up

---

[33] https://www.medicalnewstoday.com/articles/270678
[34] https://www.sciencedirect.com/topics/immunology-and-microbiology/sodium-nitrate

to 80 percent of all human cancers are driven by the effects of glucose and insulin, which stimulate the increase and spread of all types of cancer. This information is from *The Metabolic Approach to Cancer* by Dr. Nasha Winters, ND, L.A.c, FABNO and Jess Higgins Kelley, MNT. This book explains the depths of nutrition and how it can heal or destroy our livelihood. Dr. Winters was once herself a terminal cancer patient over 25 years ago, but is still thriving today due to the implementation of a healthy diet and lifestyle.

💜 **Eggs** – According to research provided from *Cleanse to Heal* by Anthony William, the proteins in eggs feed viruses, unproductive bacteria, and fungus. This dates to the 1900's when eggs were used in scientific research laboratories as food for microorganisms. These pathogens were raised on eggs in these labs and were privately categorized, patented, and censored from the outside medical system. Learn more at https://www.medicalmedium.com/

💜 **Inflammation contributing foods** – This includes lard, sodas, processed meats, refined carbs, and fried foods.

💜 **Methionine** – A recent study of breast cancer cells found that methionine deprivation reduced growth of tumor-initiating cells.[35]

Methionine is found in meat, fish, and dairy products. It is an amino acid required for cancer cell theory. The stem cell theory of cancer proposes that among all cancerous cells, a few act as stem cells that reproduce themselves and sustain the cancer, much like normal stem cells normally renew and sustain our organs and tissues.[36]

💜 **RBGH (Recombinant Bovine Growth Hormone)** – It is a lab-made growth hormone that's created using a genetic recombination DNA processes to mimic the bovine growth hormone that cows naturally produce in their bodies. It is found in milk and dairy products. While this hormone has been shown to influence the growth of tumors in some studies and may be linked to the development of prostate, colorectal, breast, and other cancers, it is still an ongoing debate. Currently RBGH is banned in Europe and Canada. In regards to the health of the cows, an EU report on the animal welfare effects of rBST states that its use often results in "severe and unnecessary pain, suffering and distress" for cows, and is "associated with serious mastitis, foot disorders and some reproductive problems."[37]

💜 "Don't Feed the Demon," is an expression I tell myself when I want to indulge knowing that certain foods and drinks are carcinogenic. However, I allow myself minimal enjoyment

35 https://www.naturalmedicinejournal.com/journal/2015-12/role-methionine-cancer-growth-and-control
36 https://med.stanford.edu/ludwigcenter/overview/theory.html
37 *Report on Animal Welfare Aspects of the Use of Bovine Somatotrophin* (PDF). The Scientific Committee on Animal Health and Animal Welfare, European Union. 10 March 1999. Archived from the original (PDF) on 4 September 2008. Retrieved 16 January 2008.

without overindulging. I don't feel that I am limiting myself, but more so that I am choosing more beneficial nourishments. From studies about alcohol and cancer risks, we see that it's best to avoid or at least limit alcohol. In correlation with alcohol and its effects on cancer, type of alcohol does not appear to matter; all alcoholic beverages include ethanol, which increases levels of acetaldehyde and in turn promotes DNA damage.[38]

💜 The impact of alcohol consumption on cancer burden differs by cancer type, and cancers of the esophagus, liver, and breast represent the most alcohol-attributable cases of cancer globally. Drinking alcohol even at lower levels of intake can increase the risk of cancer and was previously estimated that over 100,000 cases of cancer in 2020 were caused by light and moderate drinking of the equivalent of around one or two alcoholic drinks per day.[39]

💜 **BHA** – A carcinogenic, synthetic antioxidant that is used to prevent fats in foods from going rancid and as a defoaming agent for yeast. First synthesized in the late 1940's, the compound began being used as a food additive around 1947.[40]

💜 **BHT** – Triggers cancer cells. Stabilizes fats and is used to retain food smell, color and flavor. It was used as a food additive beginning in 1954.[41]

💜 **Parabens** – Chemical compound and preservative. Disrupts hormone function, which is linked to breast cancer and reproductive toxicity.[42] Found in beauty products and antiperspirants: No one wants to smell like a pungent onion, but our bodies were meant to sweat to remove toxins. Peptides produced by sweat glands act as antibiotics to fight off infection.[43] Sweating also improves mood, promotes good sleep, maintains healthy weight, and boost immunity.[44]

To avoid toxic ingredients, try natural deodorants. You can find them in most grocery stores or order them online. Keep in mind that everyone's body chemistry is different and it may take a few weeks for your body to adapt to new, natural products.

---

[38] https://jamanetwork.com/journals/jama/article-abstract/2757730

[39] https://www.mdpi.com/2072-6643/13/9/3173/htm

[40] https://www.scientificamerican.com/article/bha-and-bht-a-case-for-fresh/

[41] https://www.scientificamerican.com/article/bha-and-bht-a-case-for-fresh/

[42] https://www.scientificamerican.com/article/should-people-be-concerned-about-parabens-in-beauty-products/

[43] https://www.sciencedirect.com/topics/medicine-and-dentistry/dermcidin

[44] https://www.healthline.com/health/sweating-benefits

Here are a few natural deodorants I have tried that worked for me:

- 💜 *Alaffia Coconut Charcoal*
- 💜 *Green Goo* Aloe vera gel glide
- 💜 *Schmidt's*, with more than 10 naturally scented choices

Plant Based Diet:

Here is a list of foods and drinks to try or implement more of into your daily diet. I have found trying new foods can be fun! I enjoy visiting my local farmer's markets to explore new foods. Also knowing where my food came from gives me a sense of ease. There are so many diverse flavors to play with. If it tastes good and if it benefits your health, then wonderful!

- 💜 **Grains** – Try quinoa, brown rice, buckwheat, millet, barley, farro, amaranth, lentils, oats, spelt, sorghum, and rice cakes.
- 💜 **Legumes** – There are so many varieties of legumes to eat. To name a few; garbanzo beans, kidney beans, black beans, pinto beans, adzuki beans, navy beans, lima beans, fava beans, cannelli beans, hummus, tepary beans (high in lectins). Lectins can act as cancer cell inhibitors, which also have cancer-killing effects, targeting breast, colon and other types of cancer cells.[45] I would advise to not consume legumes if your cancer is in your organs. While the lectins can have positive results, they have also been found to cause intestinal barrier permeability and immune system dysregulation. The result may lead to organ-specific cancer development.[46]
- 💜 **Organic fruits and vegetables** – Organic fruits and veggies contain fewer pesticides. Pesticides are chemicals used for killing pests, such as rodents, insects, or plants, but can be found in our water, food, soil, and in consumer products. Pesticides can then be stored in your colon, where they slowly poison the body.[47] Although they can be more expensive, I feel it's better to spend a bit more to prevent any illnesses through nutrition. While I do not have exact proof that organic foods could have prevented any of my cancers, I'd rather not take the chance now. And the sound of eating pesticides terrifies me.

---

[45] https://www.ncbi.nlm.nih.gov/pmc/articles/PMC7245692/

[46] The Metabolic Approach to Cancer: Integrating Deep Nutrition, the Ketogenic Diet, and Nontoxic Bio-Individualized Therapies. Dr. Nasha Winters, ND, L.Ac., FABNO and Jess Higgins Kelley, MNT Chelsea Green Publishing 2017

[47] https://toxtown.nlm.nih.gov/chemicals-and-contaminants/pesticides

- 💜 **Organic teas** – Teas, especially green tea have anticancer and antibacterial effects.[48] The majority of our population is coffee drinkers. Some alternatives to coffee are Matcha green tea, chicory coffee, yerba mate, and rooibos tea which aren't as acidic.[49]
- 💜 **Fermented Foods** – Try sauerkraut, miso, olives, olive oil, and kimchi. These fermented, cultured foods provide billions of naturally occurring probiotics.[50]
- 💜 **Garlic** – Garlic is a natural antibiotic, antiviral, and contains antifungal properties while boosting the immune system.
- 💜 **Juices** – Say no to processed or store bought juices, as they are full of sugar. Instead opt for juicing fruits and vegetables or create smoothies.
- 💜 **Inflammation fighting foods** – This includes tomatoes, fruits, berries, oranges, nuts, olive oil, and leafy greens.
- 💜 **Mushrooms** – As a kid I grew up eating those little white button mushrooms. However, I was not a fan. Until recently, I had no idea the magnitude of fungi. There are so many shapes, colors, and flavors. Names of mushrooms range from Lion's Mane to Reishi to Candy Cap. See the next section for further details.

Savor Health has nutrition consultation and meal suggestions during chemotherapy that are offered from dieticians who specialize in nutrition during cancer and cancer treatments. They rely on evidence-based science published in high quality peer reviewed medical journals. https://savorhealth.com/

---

[48] Spontaneous Healing: How to Discover and Enhance Your Body's Natural Ability to Maintain and Heal Itself Andrew Weil, M.D. Published by Alfred A. Knopf New York 1995

[49] https://www.healthline.com/nutrition/coffee-alternatives

[50] The Metabolic Approach to Cancer: Integrating Deep Nutrition, the Ketogenic Diet, and Nontoxic Bio-Individualized Therapies. Dr. Nasha Winters, ND, L.Ac., FABNO and Jess Higgins Kelley, MNT Chelsea Green Publishing 2017

Fungi/Mushrooms

I'm a huge fan of adding mushrooms into my diet whether raw, cooked, powdered, or in capsule form. I strongly believe in implementing cultivated elements from nature. Be aware that there are many mushroom products out there, but you want to take the extracts made from the fruiting body as opposed to the "root" structure known as mycelium. Even though it is from the Earth, some products use fillers.

It is the Beta-glucans (key compound of a mushroom) that benefit our immune system. These substances increase host immune defense and enhance natural killer cell function.[51] There have been extensive studies on the power of fungi and more and more information is pouring out from the medical field. It's quite fascinating to read medical journals with empirical evidence highlighting the benefits of fungi.

---

[51] https://pubmed.ncbi.nlm.nih.gov/17895634/

In fact, medicinal mushrooms have been used for thousands of years in Traditional Chinese Medicine. It's just now that the United States is grasping and comprehending how effective fungi can be.

Based on what I have read from multiple sources, here are some of the best medicinal mushrooms to boost the immune system:

- 💜 Maitake
- 💜 Cordyceps
- 💜 Shiitake
- 💜 Turkey Tail
- 💜 Reishi – Contains Beta-glucans which lab studies suggest help stop the growth and spread of cancer cells.[52]

Southwest Mushrooms is a local Arizona company specializing in freshly cultivated varieties of mushrooms. Their mushrooms are beautiful and delicious! They even offer kits so that you can grow your own healing mushrooms in the convenience of your home. View one of their informational and eye-opening videos on YouTube.

https://www.youtube.com/watch?v=417Qbwn9yso#action=share
https://southwestmushrooms.com/
Email: info@southwestmushrooms.com

You may have also been hearing about the new craze of psychedelic micro-dosing. Essentially, this is the consumption of very low doses of a psychedelic substance such as psilocybin-containing mushrooms. It has been said to help improve overall mood, relieve pain, and lower anxiety (including end-of-life anxiety). Currently, the Aquilino Cancer Center in Rockville, Maryland is the only cancer center in the United States with an FDA-approved trial in psilocybin. Otherwise, psilocybin mushrooms are currently legal in Brazil, Bulgaria, Jamaica, the Netherlands, and Samoa. In the United States, however, magic mushrooms are still illegal in all 50 states. On a positive note, Denver, Colorado, became the first city in the United States to decriminalize psilocybin mushroom use. Although the drug is not legal, it is the first step in legalization. We can only hope this will become available in the very near future.[53]

---

52 https://pubmed.ncbi.nlm.nih.gov/17895634/
53 https://www.cnn.com/2019/05/08/us/denver-magic-mushrooms-approved-trnd/index.html

> *"The doctor of the future will no longer treat the human frame with drugs, but rather will cure and prevent disease with nutrition."*
>
> *—Thomas Edison*

Please venture out to try new healthy foods. You may be surprised on how delicious and diverse plant-based food can be. Here is a list of local restaurants in Arizona that offer Vegetarian, Vegan, and Gluten-free foods.

*Restaurants I highly recommend

- ♥ Giving Tree Cafe* - You will receive **$10 off your meal** as a gift from the owner, David Warr for purchasing this book.
- ♥ True Foods*
- ♥ Pomegranate Café*
- ♥ The Uprooted Kitchen*
- ♥ The Cutting Board Café*
- ♥ Ocotillo*
- ♥ Coronado
- ♥ Flower Child
- ♥ Verdura
- ♥ Luci's Marketplace (organic coffee – reopening August 2021)
- ♥ Picazzo's
- ♥ 24 Carrots
- ♥ Pita Jungle
- ♥ Seed Shack
- ♥ Desert Roots Kitchen
- ♥ Fresh Mint
- ♥ Green New American Vegetarian
- ♥ Ike's Love & Sandwiches
- ♥ Ruchi Vegetarian South Indian Cuisine

- Casa Terra (closed during the summer)
- Loving Hut
- Café Lalibela
- Veggie Village
- Vegan House
- Earth Plant Based Cuisine
- Lacuna Kava Bar – specializes in freshly brewed kava, kratom, and CBD tea
- The Joy Bus Diner – Delivers healthy meals to Cancer patients valley-wide. 100% Non-profit restaurant

Part 6

NATURAL TREATMENTS

Vitamin C infusion therapy – Published case studies report anti-cancer efficacy, improved patient well-being, and decreases in markers of inflammation and tumor growth.[54] Intravenous vitamin C for cancer therapy can decrease the toxic side effects of chemotherapy and improve quality of life.[55]

Southwest College of Naturopathic Medicine (SCNM) in Tempe, Arizona offers this infusion at about half the price of a Naturopathic clinic. https://www.scnm.edu/about/

Check with your local Naturopathic for a prescription and advice on where to go for the treatment. You will need to obtain a prescription from your doctor before receiving the infusions.

Mistletoe/Viscum injections – Reduces adverse side effects, increases overall quality of life, reduces pain, and increases survival. *Believe Big* is an organization *that helps families face, fight, and overcome cancer. The Executive Director and Co-owner Ivelisse Page,* beat the 8% survival rate of stage IV colon cancer and is completely cancer free since December 2008. https://believebig.org/

You can apply online through Believe Big's website by applying for the Wellness Grant. You must have a physician who is trained in mistletoe therapy to qualify. This will most likely be through a naturopathic physician. The grants are processed within 30 days.

Naturopathic Physicians - Rather than just suppressing symptoms, naturopathic doctors work to identify underlying causes of illness, and develop personalized treatment plans to address them. Through American Association of Naturopathic Physicians, you can find a doctor in your state. Be

---

54 https://riordanclinic.org/research-study/vitamin-c-research-ivc-protocol/
55 https://www.ncbi.nlm.nih.gov/pmc/articles/PMC6115501/

aware that most of the treatment and appointments are not covered by medical insurance. However, they can offer so much more than a traditional oncologist.

Acupuncture – Acupuncture improves circulation, enhances the flow of oxygen, and nutrients throughout the body, improves organ functions, and stimulates the nervous system to release painkillers and mood modulators. It also alleviates painful chemotherapy-related neuropathies. It suppresses nausea, vomiting, diarrhea, and constipation due to radiation and chemotherapy. If radiation has caused dry mouth, acupuncture helps by stimulating the salivary glands. It provides relief from Lymphedema by stimulating circulation to the affected area. It improves recovery after surgery, reduces hot flashes due to hormone therapy, eases fatigue, and reduces stress, anxiety, and insomnia.[56]

Check out Phoenix Community Acupuncture for a sliding scale cost between $27 to $57 per hour-long sessions. After your 10th visit, the next session is free. http://phoenixcommunityacupuncture.com/

Massage – Don't forget to pamper yourself. Massage can improve immune function, reduce pain and muscle tension, reduce stress, and help with insomnia.[57] Many schools can offer a more affordable rate as they are performed by students. You can also check with a social worker for more resources that offer affordable rates for cancer patients.

Reiki – Reiki is a Japanese technique for stress reduction and relaxation that also promotes healing through energy of the healer's hands. There is little to sometimes no touch involved as the energy force is performing the healing. According to practitioners, energy can stagnate in the body where there has been physical injury or possibly emotional pain. In time, these energy blocks can cause illness.[58] *Prana Reiki* by Kelly Greene is an incredible healing experience. She is a Certified Medical Reiki Master and Reiki Master Teacher in Phoenix, Arizona. Kelly is also certified in Crystal Healing and Sound Healing. 602.510.6720 http://pranareiki.com/index.html

Integrative treatments – Integrative Medicine (IM) is healing-oriented medicine that takes account of the whole person, including all aspects of lifestyle. It emphasizes the therapeutic relationship between practitioner and patient, is informed by evidence, and makes use of all appropriate therapies.[59] I find it

---

56 https://www.cancerhealth.com/article/betting-cure-yung-lie
57 https://www.mayoclinic.org/healthy-lifestyle/stress-management/in-depth/massage/art-20045743
58 https://www.medicalnewstoday.com/articles/308772
59 https://integrativemedicine.arizona.edu/about/definition.html

beneficial for myself to tackle my cancer from all angles. Instead of just relying on one type of treatment, IM allows me to receive treatments that are based on me as an individual.

Yoga – Multiple studies have shown that it can decrease the secretion of cortisol, the primary stress hormone. [60] Yoga has many benefits including reduction of inflammation and chronic pain, relieves anxiety, improves quality of life, and promotes sleep quality.[61]

Call Virginia G. Piper Cancer Center at 623-580-5800 to register for free classes. This is based in Arizona, but most states offer free healing courses to cancer patients.

Meditation – There's no such thing as perfect meditation. Sometimes your <u>focus</u> will wander or you'll forget to follow your breath. That's OK. It's part of the experience.[62] Research has said to help improve health problems and promote healthy behaviors. Similar to yoga, meditation can help ease anxiety and depression. [63]

[60] https://www.ncbi.nlm.nih.gov/pmc/articles/PMC4784068/
[61] https://www.healthline.com/nutrition/13-benefits-of-yoga
[62] https://www.headspace.com/meditation-101/what-is-meditation
[63] https://www.nccih.nih.gov/health/meditation-in-depth

Part 7

FURTHER READING AND RECOMMENDATIONS

*Denotes Arizona based

BOOKS:

Ani's Raw Food Kitchen Easy, Delectable Living Foods Recipes by Ani Phyo 2007 Da Capo Press

Dying to Be Me: My Journey From Cancer, To Near Death, To True Healing by Anita Moorjani 2012 Hay House, Inc.

Prepare for Surgery, Heal Faster: A Guide of Mind-Body Techniques by Peggy Huddleston 1996 Angel River Press

Radical Remission: Surviving Cancer Against All Odds by Dr. Kelly A. Turner, Ph.D. 2014 HarperCollins Publishers

Radical Hope: 10 Key Healing Factors from Exceptional Survivors of Cancer & Other Diseases by Dr. Kelly A. Turner, Ph.D. 2020 Hay House, Inc.

Spontaneous Healing by Andrew Weil, M.D. 1995 Alfred A. Knopf, Inc.

You Can Heal Your Life by Louise L. Hay 1999 Hay House, Inc.

PODCASTS/TALKS:

An Integrative Approach to Prevention, Treatment, and Healing of Cancer Love & Guts - Dr. Lise Alschuler, ND FABNO

Daily Breath with Deepak Chopra

Dr. Jonathan Stegall MD Cancer Secrets

Dr. Eric Berg DC – YouTube

Gastropod's podcast looks at food through the lens of science and history. https://gastropod.com/the-mushroom-underground/

Laura Alden Kamm The Voice of Intuition Podcast

Oprah's SuperSoul Conversations - podcast

Srikanth Kulkarni – podcast

TED talks – Paul Stamets at TEDMED 2011; How to Reduce the Side Effects of Chemotherapy

William Li TED2010; Can we eat to starve cancer?

WEBSITES:

Attacking Cancer – https://attackingcancer.org

Dr. Andrew Weil: Anti-Inflammatory Diet and Pyramid www.drweil.com

Cancer and Careers www.cancerandcareers.org

*Cancer Support Community of Arizona www.cscaz.org

Cancer Support Community www.cancersupportcommunity.org 888.793.9355

ConsumerLab – Leading provider of independent test results to help consumers and healthcare professionals identify the best quality health and nutrition products. https://www.consumerlab.com/

The Environmental Working Group (EWG) - The Dirty Dozen produce list - https://www.ewg.org/foodnews/dirty-dozen.php

Equal Employment Opportunity Commission (EEOC) 800.669.4000 www.eeoc.org

Hailey Cloud: Raw Vegan local food demonstrations - https://www.livingrawbygrace.com/about-me.html

*My Hope Bag – Provides free bags filled with helpful goodies and support services for women with breast cancer in the state of Arizona www.myhopebag.org

LawHelp www.lawhelp.org

National Coalition for Cancer Survivorship (NCCS) www.canceradvocacy.org

Patient Advocate Foundation 800.532.5274 www.patientadvocate.org

Virginia G. Piper Cancer Care Network at Honor Health facilities – support groups and health programs https://www.honorhealth.com

HEAL documentary on Netflix – After viewing this show I was beyond inspired and filled with hope. This then led to me purchasing the book, *Radical Remission,* as listed in my recommended book section.

ACKNOWLEDGEMENTS

Many thanks to all those who have donated money for publication of this book. I am so grateful for all the support from family, friends, and strangers in making this book possible. Thank you to Kinley Donaldson for the wonderful illustrations. Another thanks to Megan Fox and Nika Levikov for their tireless hours editing my book from the very beginning. To those that have chosen to read my book, I also thank you for being brave and strong-willed, knowing that you can heal yourself.

Every breath is a gift. Focus on living.

_____